UNLEARNING LEADERSHIP

UN

LEARNING
LEADERSHIP

KNOW YOURSELF—
GROW YOUR BUSINESS

GUY BELL

LIGHT BODY

UNLEARNING LEADERSHIP
Know Yourself - Grow Your Business

ISBN   978-1-5445-0082-9 *Paperback*
        978-1-5445-0083-6 *Ebook*

CONTENTS

The time has come to explore the wild idea that we are better off together than apart. It's time we release our limiting beliefs for a taste of the truth beyond our beliefs.

IMPORTANT DISCLOSURE

I've been fortunate in my career to work in start-up, publicly traded, and private-equity-backed companies. Each of these experiences helped form the content of *Unlearning Leadership*. However, none of the lessons I will share with you is about any individual leader or company. When I write about a CEO, executive, or "the company," the stories are a reflection of many leaders and companies. In most cases, the stories are true across the board.

To this end, most of the leaders I've worked with over the years were smart. Several, in my observation, were brilliant. Precious few had the ability to get beyond "being smart" to meet the companies' full potential. They were stuck in a school of thought that limited them and everyone around them.

This book is meant to challenge the "smart" leader and expand the "heart" leader. This book is in honor of those teachers that taught me what not to do, and what to do.

THE END OF BUSINESS AS USUAL

A business friend was recently trying to convince me that I needed to *rightsize* my ambition to change the world. She suggested I have two problems in my approach. The first is that I believe business has the single greatest potential to do good in our world. She actually said, "Are you effin' kidding me?" And the second is that change happens incrementally, person to person. It will not happen systemically. She couldn't leave it at her opinion so she added, "Duh!"

"Really?" I went on to say, "When we change the way we do business around the world, we change the world. One and a billion are the same! I don't understand your desire to impact one life when all of life would benefit from the same experience."

Business leaders are notoriously disinterested in the

human condition. They're taught to trust in a school of thought that says, "it's *not* personal, it's *just* business." And then they focus on managing up, driving results, and protecting the business from unwarranted risk. To counteract this, human resource departments often design systems meant to make people feel good about their job and the company.

I say it *is* personal and it's *not* just business. Changing this *school of thought* will begin the journey of unlearning leadership to capture all the unmet potential of actually caring.

My friend and millions like her believe in another school of thought that suggests people are one of the primary challenges in business. They hold this elite view that some people are born leaders and the rest are born followers. Their notion of a good employee is one who does what they're told.

This limited thinking is "driving" business results that are mediocre—and I say this is crazy! Why wouldn't every single leader rethink their approach to achieve their full business potential by engaging in the full human potential? Ricardo Semler and Richard Branson, among other unconventional leaders, have broken the mold. They are setting a new course in the age beyond *business as usual*.

What are you waiting for? Is it too much of a risk to be

yourself and trust people? Perhaps it's too much of a "leap of faith" to fully engage in the human potential. Seems too "out there." You trust in results, results, results!

It is anything but "out there" to pursue excellence through a complete embrace of the real power within each human being. Unleash the full potential of every person and you will grow your business in all the ways you currently measure growth and more. When you unlearn the endless limiting schools of thought about leadership, you will find yourself thinking.

This distinction is important. Thinking requires a clear mind, open to all the possibilities, and then a creative mind to accurately use the requisite data. Decisions often become less about being right and more about doing what is right.

A school of thought keeps most people from thinking. In place of being present and thinking without any predetermined answers, people use models, methods, and measurements from the same or similar data that are often incomplete or, worse, inaccurate. And when the data are accurate, many leaders attempt to skew the data to support what they want it to say.

At the core, thinking freely is letting go of what you "know" to allow room for what you don't know. This state of presence accelerates your curiosity and invites others into the critical and creative processing. In this place of intellectual freedom, you grow and everyone around you grows.

This is my call to *action*. I'm going to challenge you to *act* on this potential awaiting you and the world of business. Some of what you'll read will make sense to your business logic and some of it won't. I'll do my best to frame it all in a way that you can relate to the insights and trust enough to consider another point of view.

On balance, there are going to be *actions* you will need to take that may or may not be easily accepted. And in some cases, you will simply not be prepared to accept the challenge of becoming a transformative leader of a transformative company. This resistance is normal for all of us.

I'm open to debating the merits, helping contextualize the value specifically for you or your organization, and doing damn near anything I can to help you reframe your business and rethink your approach as long as you stay open.

My goal is simple: to change the world by changing the way we approach business. I've used the saying "the business of life becomes the life of business." I'm not sure if this is the right "pointer" to simplify the next hundred-plus pages for the sake of remembering the essence of what is written, versus memorizing a system or steps to an outcome. But I am certain that life is our great teacher. Natural systems always win. When we understand our business's "ecosystem," we make smarter, more sustainable decisions.

If you're like me, you may be saying, "Who has time to allow for natural systems to catch up with the speed of today's business demands? Investors and customers have no patience." We have co-created this idea of what people "want." When you keep asking why, you will often end up with a mess of incongruent desires. This will not be a fast or slow transition.

Or you may want to use the acronym ACT: Accelerate, Co-create, Transform. There will be a few more simple ideas that hold the wisdom we all have within ourselves. In this case, we are all accelerators, wired to co-create and connect with the transformative nature of life itself.

I see these as anchoring for the sake of tapping into a deeper knowing: a place beyond our business beliefs, which are currently anchoring us in limiting business norms. The anchor you choose will define the outcome.

My business successes have come from a relentless pursuit of excellence. Nothing new here. Everyone I know says this, and precious few I know actually invest in what it takes to be excellent. So, it makes sense to start off the book with a few points of difference. Before I do, one distinction: I'm not talking about personal peak performance. There are wonderful lessons around the idea of "fast forwarding," a concept where peak performers visualize a future state before it is realized. Many of our great athletes have mastered this practice, which is a pointer to excellence in business, yet applied differently.

To set the stage, excellence requires being fully engaged in the human condition. Contrary to current thinking, people are not replaceable parts. Success over time requires fully realized human beings expressing themselves fully in the business. Regardless of whether every person is in the right position and fully engaged today, your leadership can have a life-changing impact when you "go first." You lead! You humanize! You care.

It starts with you! Every single person counts, and the leader that is bestowed with the role of guiding the vision, or whatever words are used, has to be *all in! All in* on getting to know how she must shift to her "whole-body wisdom" (WBW)—yes, I wrote WBW and will unpack this at the end. No need to be distracted by this way of "knowing." The business stories I use to illustrate our current broken business ideas will demonstrate the need to go beyond the ego and limiting schools of thought. WBW is one way of describing what is beyond our oversized egoic selves. This new thinking still requires the leader to use her amazing mental capacity, but only as a tool.

All in will mean being present within and throughout the organization to set the tone for a human-centric experience. And *all in* means you can no longer get away with surface beliefs to make people *feel* like you or the company cares. The idea of caring through nice words and an over-the-top human resources push isn't the answer. You either care or you don't. All or nothing!

Another key difference is addressing how the business operates. I'll fire off a handful of the norms that have to change. Some of these will be covered in the book. They are: creating "separation" and distrusting "others," hiring based on "qualifications," using policies to correct behavior, using buzzwords to gloss over reality, focusing on investors as the primary stakeholders, unnecessarily building layers of management, overmanaging when things are tough, breeding a lack of intellectual diversity, attempting to "design" culture through ideas like "transparency," building a hero culture that encourages people to become "arsonists" and "firefighters," managing to numbers as an input, using incomplete data to make decisions, completely lacking an understanding of risk and innovation, and the list goes on...

Hopefully you get the point.

As you dive into the book, I will start off with a framework I call the **Four Rules of Flight**. This will take shape as another way to simplify the complexity of transforming how we run business for the good of all!

From here, I will pick up on **Two Ideas** about what is missing in our lives today. We talk about "other" people like they are less than we are *and* we overreact to life when "Because" will suffice. We are in this together and nothing is good or bad. Both of these lessons can be translated into all the roles we play. By believing in separation and judging things that happen, we limit potential.

The final section will be about you. **It Starts with You**. Your inner journey to unlearn old patterns and relearn new ones will tap into your *felt sense* or your WBW. From this awareness, you will *act* in alignment with your potential. Getting to "yes" in a world of "no" comes from how you think, feel, and respond to everything you do.

This section will give you pointers to "do the work" if you are motivated by this approach. Or you may prefer the approach of "letting go to know." However you get your head and heart around the fact, you are removing layers of completely incongruent beliefs and practices for the sake of reaching your full potential. As you grow into this awareness, so grows everyone around you. The only way to know this is to let go. And *holy crap* is that hard for *everyone*, and, I would suggest, harder for those of you who have been wildly successful.

Each section will begin with the three circles above, as a reminder of how the book is structured.

Before we dive into these three stories, I will share some ideas about the source of business successes.

WHAT IS THE SOURCE OF BUSINESS WISDOM?

Although there are undoubtedly many amazing professors teaching beyond a school of thought, education is not the *source* of wisdom in business.

In fact, it is a part of perpetuating limiting beliefs.

Learning how to learn is important.

Learning how to unlearn is required.

And learning to think with your whole-body wisdom is a game changer.

Of the many successful authors selling another school of thought, most are repeating a different version of the same thing. Innovation simply isn't in the DNA of "business as usual." The leaders able to transform their businesses have abandoned business norms and left the comfort of needing to feel in control or certain.

A few of my favorite teachers are an idealist from Seattle, a rebel from Brazil, and an academic from Cambridge University.

Dee Hock coined a term, "chaordic leadership," by combing "chaos" and "order." His explanation of the term is as follows: "By *chaord*, I mean any self-organizing, self governing, adaptive, nonlinear, complex organism, organization, community or system, whether physical, biological or social, the behavior of which harmoniously blends characteristics of both chaos and order."[*] He quietly created one of the most ubiquitous brands in the world: Visa. This international organization grew out of this self-organizing approach. It has since become like every other large corporate structure, but not until it scaled the heights of a massive worldwide business.

Ricardo Semler, CEO of Semco Partners, has been speaking to Ivy League MBA students for decades about his

---

[*] Dee Hock, "The Art of Chaordic Leadership," Meadowlark Institute, accessed April 27, 2018. http://www.meadowlark.co/the_art_of_chaordic_leadership_hock.pdf

business. And his business model is one of a kind. Yet no one is buying his offer to help them create their version of his business model.

Sugata Mitra proved that a child-centered education was a better way to get results. He went to the poorest, least-educated areas of the world and, over time, proved his theory. Being an academic, he went through the long and arduous process of proving his assumptions in a unique and compelling way. Once he had all the data to show the world another way, he offered his services to help anyone interested. Few people are taking him up on this offer.

These three "thought leaders" have taught us how to innovate by throwing out the old ideas and starting anew. Elon Musk is another trailblazer worthy of our time. In his case, we are giving him more attention than the previous examples. This is either a sign of the times or a result of the proliferation of media coverage. Or both.

Regardless of where the universe of writers sit as they attempt to influence leaders, organizations, and innovators, precious few of the transformative ideas are adopted.

Getting an education in business is perfectly fine and can prepare graduates to fit into the business world as it is. Reading books to learn about an idea or another nuance to being an Effective Executive (Peter Drucker) is fine.

In my experience, the *source* of wisdom isn't found in a school of thought, regardless of the bent. In fact, it really isn't found at all. The source of wisdom in business is *experienced*. When we open up to all *experiences*, the source, or experience, will reveal more than we can know. By allowing the natural wisdom to unfold, our intellect is used as a tool rather than relied on as rule, a school of thought.

Being a student of life means you are paying attention to all living systems, to include yourself and those around you. In this state of wonder, you are in the most complex classroom, which is waiting for you to interact with it. You are observing, inquiring, connecting, and disconnecting. You are debating, deliberating, testing, and failing. You are curious, persistent, yet patient.

You come alive! You are engaging in whatever life is presenting.

This state of *being present* in the "isness" of life, in the fractal nature of systems, will teach you critical thinking when you start to critically observe and play. You will learn from everyone and everything around you because you are in the moment. You now are beginning to experience the *source*.

Unfortunately, most of us rely heavily on a school of thought and our intellectual acuity. These trusted sources have defined generations of leaders. We've numbed our-selves into believing this is "the way things work." Leaving this comfort of what we think we know for a taste of the unknown isn't going to come easy.

As impossible as it may seem, you are trading endless potential for certainty. My hope is that you will play with the idea that *Unlearning Leadership* holds the most potential for your personal growth and, in turn, your business growth.

In choosing what appears to be certainty, you are deny-ing endless potential for yourself and your business. Think again!

I'm going to count down the problems of business in four steps. I'll begin by structuring the rules as they are in business today, and then show you what is possible when you unlearn the way things are, in favor of the open field of the way things *actually are* or ought to be!

Note: I don't have "the answer" to the limitless ways the life of your business expresses its potential. I have, however, learned that in the powerful acceptance of unlearning leadership, you will begin to experience the life of your business. And, in turn, your business will become a more transformative environment.

There are four rules of flight. Starting with the rules as they are today means I'll start at Four. I'll then count down to One. I'll describe each lesson on the way down. I will then rebuild the way things "ought to be" by starting with One and moving back to Four.

In truth, the numbers are irrelevant. Start wherever you are and with whichever area you need the most work. One is the best place to start if you haven't been indoctrinated into the cult of Four.

The linear nature of numbers and moving up or down a scale is an important part of this story. The essence of life is nonlinear, chaotic, and agile, yet fractal. Business systems are linear, ordered, and controlled, and therefore limiting. Although there are many companies that have designed outstanding systems with the requisite complexity, most systems are limited by people's desire for control—a subtle difference that makes all the difference!

Life doesn't work in a neat package. As I wrote earlier,

my goal is to create a few ways of simplifying what is otherwise a fairly complex problem. My goal is to simplify without dumbing it down. Let's dive in!

You never change things by fighting the existing reality. To change something, build a new model that makes the existing model obsolete.

—BUCKMINSTER FULLER

FOUR RULES OF FLIGHT

Weight, lift, thrust, and drag.

Business today: Most leaders spend their time building and managing systems, processes, and rules. They invest the majority of the company's time developing, maintaining, updating, and managing to the "rules."

The desire to control behaviors, activities, interactions, and outcomes is possibly the greatest undiagnosed addiction in human history. I know, I'm overstating the point. Or am I?

In the practice of Four, our lives are valued as consumers. Our work is valued on the basis of a return on investment. Our human value is defined by how well we "play our role" or "fall into line." Although these definitions are universal, once in management, two primary expectations emerge: to "drive performance" and to be politically savvy. The irony of "driving performance" in a world of debilitating rules, inconsistent expectations, and fear is that nothing aligns with the stated desire to maximize performance. Fear is the key driver.

So why do leaders keep up this charade?

It works! At least long enough to take the money and run!

As leaders grow in their career, they toggle between playing politics and mastering the art of outcomes. I'd say "science," but most use fear and favor to get what they want. And what they want is to look good. This eventually equates to outcomes. They begin to learn the fine art of political positioning to manage expectations from above. And in this process, they slowly lose their natural instincts to connect people with performance.

This dance continues until, voilà, they've made it to the top. Now their life is all about politics. Results remain a part of the political game, but only in terms of the art of "reasoning."

We're simply humans judging other humans' "worth" on the basis of all kinds of screwed-up beliefs and business concepts. Most of this misguided thinking happens in Four.

Fear thrives in a continual cycle of reacting to negative news. The downside of how natural systems often work is that resistance creates more resistance. This cycle creates the need to add new rules, fire "bad actors," and hire more "cops." Before you know it, your whole business is a trap of sorts.

Most leaders have *arrived* by playing with the executive "school of thought" and simply cannot move off the game plan of following those who got them there. Even if it's not the actual people that got them there, since the club is fairly prescriptive, the allegiance is to the norms. So they continue with the old school of thought by putting on more elaborate masks with each promotion. Each rung on the ladder often equals a kind of acceptance to die to their "self." And then one fine day, everyone in the system is a corporate robot, including those at the top.

This state of running our companies from a Four mindset has its value. Building well-designed systems and developing an agile process for exceptional customer service happens in Four. Growing your business to scale is also a highly valuable attribute of Four.

Because most companies live their entire business lives in Four, they seldom if ever develop past their self-imposed limitations. These limitations come when leaders start creating policies to correct behavior. Or when they hire lawyers to manage compliance and risk. In the extreme, they hire the top consulting companies to build a "human capital strategy" or an "innovation model" to structure a way to keep the right people and get them to be creative within the model.

If it's not obvious why this doesn't work, I hope it becomes obvious as you read on.

To illustrate what I'm talking about, I'll describe how this penchant to makes rules for seemingly everything and create policies to correct behaviors kills potential.

Before I dive into examples of Four thinking in business, I want to cover one of the essential building blocks of this mindset. *Systems* are at the heart of everything we do. Our education system, healthcare system, and business systems in general all serve this foregone conclusion that systems are the backbone of these sectors.

But, in fact, systems are designed as a reaction to something rather than as a solution. I can hear many of you saying, "there's no distinction between these two points."

A system, done well, is designed to connect people with people through products and services (generally speaking). Staying focused on the fewest rules and steps is the key. No more and no less. We see an actual need that demands a solution. Unfortunately, this isn't how we design, and then over time, add to, systems.

Case in point: A two-billion-dollar-plus company with several brands made the decision to create a centralized support system for all brands. The goal was to save money and increase service levels.

They hired one of the top consulting firms to analyze the systems within each separate business. Their objective was to find commonalities that they could leverage into a "shared services" support structure and develop the systems with the company leaders.

Outcome: The system failed on both fronts. It wasn't more efficient. In fact, the decisions played a role in crippling the company and the service levels got worse, and in many cases were a complete disaster, with two exceptions. Can you guess what the characteristics of the two exceptions were? Yup. The two were perfect choices for shared services because they were naturally suited to be "centralized."

These young, talented people recommended a variety of solutions that, on the surface, seemed logical. The company ran with the solutions, in pursuit of the cost savings. Although many of the executives argued against any shared services that were not generated from their business systems, they ended up giving in. More unfortunate was the lack of critical thinking with an eye on the priority: the customer experience.

All human-made systems grow like cancer. Most newly developed systems designed with good intentions struggle because of our penchant to add steps for internal controls without keeping the customer experience at the forefront. Designing systems for something is really hard to get right. Designing systems to protect you from something doesn't solve anything.

Well-designed systems have a few common factors. They are designed to improve the experience of all people impacted by the system and to increase certainty for all people impacted by the system. No more, no less! Thus, four rules of flight. Not three and not five. Four!

EXAMPLES
HIRING BASED ON QUALIFICATIONS

Do you filter résumés based on the level of degree, years of experience, or geography? Have you created an interview template to ensure consistency around one or two theories of how to interview? Do you use a personality profile to predict future success?

When you meet one of the top three candidates (of course,

the number is irrelevant), you ask the candidate to walk you through her résumé. She does, and half the interview is done. What did you learn? That she is articulate? Knows how to do what you are hiring her to do? Has a balance of self-awareness around times she made mistakes and confidence around her successes?

What if you knew you were missing the right candidate because you were checking the box? Would you change the way you approach attracting and hiring people? I'm going to say "yes" for you.

MY TAKE

The first questions I ask in all interviews are personal. I want to know who you are and what you love to do, and learn where you want to go in life. I couldn't care less if the answer has anything to do with the business or position. I only want to know what makes you wake up. This conversation has to be genuine. If not, it will turn out like the "interview guidelines" turn out: shallow.

"In the event we work together, I am going to help you get where you want to go. If it is within the company or something completely different, I will work to support you." Some version of this expression shows up.

I then ask questions about how you bring this passion

to work. Or, when the passions match, we talk about a variety of ways to expand. As we talk about expansion, I extend the opportunity for you to contribute to solving company-wide challenges as well as position-related gaps.

The time is really about getting to know each other, our passions in life, and our shared interest in making a difference. These conversations go where they go and take us both to a place that isn't scripted. In a state of presence, each story reveals a deeper understanding of the "match."

The trouble with trusting your instincts is that we are taught a school of thought or, worse, many schools of thought, about interviewing. For those who do trust their instincts and choose not to follow the script, they often lie to avoid getting in trouble. They tell managers what they want to hear versus telling them the truth. If they said what they thought, it would sound something like this: "I don't follow the stupid policies about hiring or scripts. The notes I take are to satisfy management. And I lie to you when questioned about the candidates' ability to meet expectations, and the proof that they can drive performance, and blah blah blah."

Now for the truth! Hiring right is an input. Culture is an input. The start of being who you are as a business and a leadership team is the beginning of a great hiring and retention process. Interviewing is relationship-building and storytelling. Within this dialogue, great interviewing explores the layers of any experience to include some important business stories.

The key to hiring right is knowing what hiring the "right person" means. The really easy part of this answer is knowing they are able to do the day-to-day work. The hard part is gaining a deeper understanding of their ability to expand. Go beyond the job. Think critically and kindly. If you profess to be an "open door" company, and when the person starts they realize you are a "closed door" company (closed people), you're screwed. Any platitude misses the mark. And everyone, over time, can see it.

This is the primary problem with all hiring. Employers are dissatisfied with employees, and employees are dissatisfied with employers.

Break the cycle. You have to know who *you—self and company—are* to hire "right." And you have to know that regardless of how good you are at knowing your story, listening to their story, and starting off on the right track, life happens. Do not attach to the outcome. And do not, I repeat, *do not* track employee attrition as a measurement of success or failure.

CREATING POLICIES TO CORRECT BEHAVIORS

In business and in life, we are addicted to creating rules in response to "bad behaviors." This addiction is accepted as normal and reinforced throughout society. But what is it accomplishing? Are we really getting better outcomes through more policies, rules, laws, and governance?

However we got to this place of believing that by creating rules designed to stop unwanted behaviors we have solved a problem, we are wrong!

This lesson points to overmanaging kids, partners, employees, and societies. And, no surprise, some of us overmanage ourselves. Every system has about the same misunderstanding of its desire to curb risk by creating barriers to taking risks. I'm opening up multiple channels for you to explore, beyond what I'll focus on here.

BUSINESS

Have you ever made a bad purchase and, after using the product, gone back to the store and heard, "I'm sorry, I'm not approved to accept returns that have been used"? Who is? And I'm curious, how would I know how my feet felt in the shoes had I not worn them for the day? Or the employee points to the sign in front of the register that describes the no-return policy. This song and dance is the orchestration of some misguided corporate person crunching numbers to mitigate the risk of financial loss on returns.

However they measured the decision, they missed the single point of failure. Build a business with your target customer in mind. Measure everything and allow the messiness of bad behaviors by both the customer and employee to be what it is. The great employees far outweigh the weak ones and the same holds true of customers.

When you have a product returned, and you decide to figure out the cost to the company of changing the bad behavior of returning used product by creating a new policy, think again. If you don't want to figure in the cost of returns, then you'd better figure out a way to treat your honest customer well. Meaning, run your company to serve the behaviors you want, and continue building on trusting relationships. The same holds true for your team and community.

I recently purchased a shirt from Marine Layer. In my struggle to pick the "right color," this awesome young woman said, "You have a year to figure out if that's the right color." Shocked by the statement, I said, "Don't you know I'm the customer, and you're supposed to treat me like I don't matter? What's wrong with you!" We laughed. She was cool, in part, because the owners gave her the freedom to be cool. Needless to say, I'm now a devoted part of the Marine Layer community.

How do we, as rational people, get to this place where we become the bureaucratic system that forces mediocrity?

Start-ups tend to get this right. They have policies for third-party requirements, but not for their internal actions. As they grow, bad behaviors and decisions emerge, and the start-up responds with—you got it—a new policy to counteract the behavior. This habit continues to spiral until they end up like the majority of large companies, blocking their employees from helping the customers.

My rule of thumb is this: Never create a policy to correct behavior. Be discerning and protect the health of your organization from the fear of mistakes. The more we allow this insidious creep of policies, the closer we are to killing our business.

Instead of bureaucracy and policies, focus on removing the barrier for your team to take the right actions. The penchant to punish is a dangerous friend to protecting the company from people. Instead, protect the company from itself.

TRANSPARENCY

We've all heard "transparency" in buzzword bingo, but that hasn't created anything resembling true transparency. We invest in lawyers to help us become more transparent, but they use compliance as the gateway to transparency and it misses the mark.

I was recently in an executive meeting that was ominously held behind closed doors. One of the first comments made by the CEO was, "This conversation can't leave the room."

I watched as a room full of smart people aggressively defended their beliefs around a range of topics that didn't need the closed-door approach. Most of the conversation had no real tangible business value, with one exception. And that exception was some positive news. Since that was the only positive takeaway, I decided to share it with my team when I got back to the office. The next morning, I attended an emergency call with the cadre of executives, and the call started with an unveiled threat about sharing the content of our closed-door meeting.

I immediately said that they didn't need to conduct an investigation and that I had shared what I had experienced as inspiring news. I didn't realize that positive news had been the reason for closing the door. In this case, everyone supported my decision. But in far too many cases, no good deed goes unpunished.

Either be transparent and then invite others to practice the same, or don't. Everyone or no one. And when you have to keep secrets, keep the secrets. But know the difference.

I started to co-write a book in early 2000 that mocked the vacuous management catch-phraseology of the day. In the process of talking about our own experiences, I learned about "buzzword bingo." And I'd thought we were the first to market. Oh well! The bingo words go something like this: "results driven," "synergy," "empowerment," "think outside the box," "team player," "A player," "big data," and so on. We had a long list of buzzwords and a few sayings to boot. My timeless favorites are "We need to get buy-in on this," "You have to drive the results," and "What is the ROI?" The overall winner for me remains, "I want our employees to feel like we care about them."

When I heard this statement for the first time, I was shocked. In a state of wonder, I asked, **"Why not just care about them?"** Over my years of asking this question to underscore the contrast between caring and the idea of caring, many leaders were puzzled. After the initial answer, I would probe more deeply, and though it was as clear as day to me and most employees, it remained a useless distinction to the top leaders.

We didn't get too far on the book before we were captured by the demands of our growing careers. I started to pay more attention to my language and realized I'd become one of *them*. The book suddenly felt disingenuous. I also started to realize I had my version of what mattered, and as much as I wanted to believe my cult of ideas was better, it wasn't necessarily objectively true.

This started me down the path of exploring why business leaders were obsessed with culture as an expression of the thoughts of a few "thought leaders" (another buzzword-bingo term). I began paying close attention to my experiences in various executive roles, with some research sprinkled in.

Over the next seventeen years I expanded my buzzword vocabulary by sitting on boards, working with publicly traded businesses and equity-backed investments. My favorite experiences were closed-door conversations that "never left the room": rooms full of people bouncing between a more sophisticated bingo game and raw aggression.

My conclusion: culture is a reflection of the whole "tribe" (a newer bingo word). Defining culture to create an outcome isn't culture. It's akin to creating a policy to correct a behavior. In the short run, you may get the desired behaviors in both cases, but you won't get what you're truly interested in. In these more candid conversations, I found a deeper truth. This deeper truth, albeit unspoken outside the room, was the actual culture.

Culture is a reflection of outcome, much like the bottom

line. Yet most businesses manage it as an input, and when they do, everything they do to "drive" business creates friction. **This friction "drives" people away because they are being sold crap rather than being engaged in the experience of running the business.** They start to check out, get sick more frequently, do just enough, and play along for now or, worse, for a lifetime. They start playing buzzword bingo. All this is due to a lack of trust—a lack of being connected to something greater than a job.

I suggest considering the following two ideas as a path forward.

Idea for employees: Start with yourself! How do you wake up today and choose to do the hard work of "showing up"? You choose to act in alignment with your full potential by holding yourself accountable. You check your ego at the door and become an owner of the business. You invest in making the business better day in and day out, regardless of whether the company, culturally, is a freaking mess or not. You have a choice today. You *accept* what is, you *stay curious* and seek to understand and actively engage, or you *depart*. Departing is fine when the culture or job doesn't work for you. Choose to show up no matter what, or choose to go. Don't wait for someone else to choose for you.

Idea for executives: It starts with you! If you really want to attract and keep outstanding people, *do it*. Run the business *with* every person. Engage *with* every person by having the fewest layers keeping people from people. When the business requires people telling people telling people what to do, you have to figure out how you will avoid ass-covering. Not easy to do from a list of words and abstract conversations; achievable when you embody and extend the invitation for all others to embody this kind of investment in each other. Accept the fact that you, my friend, are not that important. And yet, you are vitally important.

The slowest path to building a transformative culture is to rely on every individual person choosing to *act* as the owner, regardless of the cultural mess.

The fastest path to building a transformative culture is to *be* a transformational CEO or executive. Here's the simple part: all you have to do is be *yourself*. If you're like most of the executives I've worked for and with, you think you are already internally aligned. Stop thinking. You likely are not!

Culture matters! It is simply the expression of how close we are to or how far away we are from our full potential.

Words count! Use meaningful language to express your actual beliefs.

Avoid using clichés!

THREE IDEAS THAT WILL CHANGE EVERYTHING

Thoughts become things.

Words that aren't aligned with thoughts dilute action.

Actions that aren't aligned with thoughts and words silently destroy businesses.

In business today: Very few business leaders are aligned top to bottom. When they are, the business, for better or worse, is aligned with their beliefs.

Be careful to examine what you're thinking so you align your words and actions with your thoughts. What you think about or believe is *key*! To this end, be aware of your thoughts before you align them with words and actions. Get ready to unlearn and relearn how you think. That is, if you want to meet your full potential in life and business.

I have seldom experienced healthy alignment in business. Since I'm endlessly curious about how other businesses operate, I talk with as many people as I can about their business experiences. This gap holds true across sectors and sizes of organizations.

When your thoughts match your words, and your actions support what you say and do, the likelihood of success increases. Unfortunately, the lessons shared in Four are born of having limiting thoughts that show up in limiting words and play out in the actions of the business by running the business from fear.

Alignment, good or bad, is better than misalignment.

Would you rather have an outstanding idea that is poorly executed or a decent idea that is well executed? This line of questioning is good, but needs a refresh.

My version: Would you rather own a "unicorn" business that captures the imagination of the moment *or* build a business focused on life-changing products or services with a team of passionate believers?

If your answer is "Duh! I'm *in* on fast wealth; get in, get out; or run up and exit," that is perfectly fine. Getting rich quick is a high. Getting to market dominance quickly is attractive. Getting out fast to do it again is OK.

If your answer is "Duh! Why would anyone make money for the sake of money?" you are hired! Another positive view of the situation is "Making a difference and creating wealth and opportunity is where I want to be!"

Back to the premise of Three. Know what you believe! Even if you are proud of being an ass to people. When you are an aligned ass with narcissistic tendencies, you will improve performance by attracting people that, for some reason, want to be around people like you. You want people that accept your flavor of driving people. I'd prefer that you work on your limiting beliefs for the good of yourself and everyone around you. If you do, you will have a shot at creating a transformational business.

EXAMPLES

THINKING OR MACHINE THINKING?

My belief is that right action happens in the right time. The right unifying purpose will inspire right action on every level of the organization. Speed matters, but not for the sake of speed.

In contrast, machine thinking is our enemy! Getting things done to get things done is the enemy of creativity. And creativity is the enemy of stagnation. Choose sides!

Far too many leaders choose the wrong side, and everyone, in the end, pays for their mistake!

Have you been a Whole Foods customer? Were you a satisfied and delighted customer? (Whole Foods values a bunch of things, one of which is to satisfy and delight you.) How about Amazon? I have been a customer of both companies for a few decades now and want to share my personal experience with each and how this has mirrored their growth.

John Mackey, CEO and founder of Whole Foods, has a real passion for his creation. Amazon CEO Jeff Bezos has masterfully unified his company around an enduring belief he coined "First Day." This simple and brilliant obsession is alive and well in much of the Amazon culture, so I'm told, and my experience as a consumer suggests this is true. Why? The business, since Day One, has been about *me*. Their vision is to be the earth's most customer-centric company.

Why, you may ask, am I bringing up these two companies? For one, Amazon recently purchased Whole Foods. And Whole Foods lost its way over time, while Amazon continues to thrive. So what happened to Whole Foods?

I know of some of the dysfunction that grew over time, through talking to passionate employees sharing their experiences. To be fair, I can get the same anecdotal evidence by doing the same with Amazon or any company. My point isn't to attack John or overstate the negative. There is an important contrast.

Back to the point. Unfortunately, John Mackey believed the opposite of what my friends experienced. He was quoted as saying that the company valued its employees over the customer and he believed this played a part in their decline. Those employees I knew over the years lived a very different experience. The company they all felt committed to in the early years didn't exist any longer. My shopping experience followed the story my friends shared.

As a customer in the nineties, I enjoyed going to the store as much as I did shopping there. The experience, unfortunately, shifted over time. It was no longer an experience, and other grocers expanded into this space with a better price and experience. Contrary to what Mackey says, they turned into a *machine-thinking* business that devalued people: both their employees and customers.

To be fair, most businesses scale poorly because they don't have enduring vision that can unify a large dispersed workforce. In the absence of this visionary call to action and an easy set of values or operating expectations, companies scale by adding more and more rules with less and less autonomy. They increase layers of management to inspect for consistency and ensure everyone is doing their job.

Eventually, the customer becomes a nuisance because they are no longer a part of the conversation. Everyone is too busy covering their ass to care. Talented people leave and tired people stay, in fear of losing their job. I call this machine thinking and Bezos calls this Day Two.

Why do two businesses, both with real market value, end up in extremely different places? Leadership! Vision! This may seem out of place when looking at the two founder CEOs side by side. Mackey seems to have an authentic drive to do well by doing good. In the beginning years, his voice inspired the troops. But he didn't have an enduring vision that scaled. Bezos was, and has always been, relentlessly focused, and he never lost track of his vision.

More people solving for the best customer experience creates the best customer experience. Fewer people solving for the best customer experience means fewer satisfied customers. Pretty simple.

DESIGNING CULTURE

Culture is an outcome.

By focusing on Three versus Four, you can begin to unwind the practices of designing culture for the authentic experience you and your team co-create. This will happen day in and day out when you align your thoughts and words, and ACT from a unified place.

An aligned business can Accelerate without overmanaging, because people are Co-creating with our great teacher: life. Life itself is Transformative! Transforming how we do business requires us to be present. In this presence, we will be able to maintain Three, regardless of the ups and downs life throws our way.

Let go of the notion that you control other people. Regardless of how well-intentioned your desire may be, manipulating people to get what you want is a fool's game. And no one needs to be a fool or be fooled into anything.

Start anywhere with the lesson, and it will impact everything in your life and your business.

DRIVING RESULTS

Results are an outcome.

This lesson feels like I'm insulting everyone reading this book, but, in my experience, it is universally true that *we* manage to results. Oddly, this belief is true all the way up to CEOs and boards. Our misguided behaviors have us believing that we drive the results of other people. In fact, when the business grows and we add multiple layers of middle and upper management, we have people driving people to drive other people to hit a number. What a colossal waste of time!

Results are earned through relationships. Results are earned through discipline. Results are earned by caring.

Can you get results through fear? Yes! Can you get results through stating the obvious? Yes! Can you make a career out of telling people to try harder and retire with little or no knowledge about how results are earned? Yes!

This is exactly why precious few people do anything different. They don't need to or are not asked to take a different approach. We are dumbing down really smart people to this level of learned incompetence.

Results are about relationships. Results are earned through discipline and care. Results are reliant on a team executing flawlessly and together. They are a way to reflect on what did and didn't work this time around.

And for the record, we drive cars. We earn results. We don't drive people.

IT TAKES TWO

*Everyone deserves your full
attention, including you!*

*Be present with each person and you will
become connected with all people!*

*Share what you know, and listen
for what you don't know!*

In business today: The truth that each person counts is simply not in our current school of thought. The executive playbook states that leaders should create the perception they care. Actually caring enough to accept that each person matters is a sign of weakness.

We are simply "too busy" to care about each person, let alone talk to each person about the business. Given this general belief, the higher you get on the organizational chart, the smarter you are, and therefore the less you need from "your employees." Your attitude toward "others" is that you've been there, done that, and don't need to hear another person complain about one thing or another. You've heard it all!

The truth: You don't have employees. You work with other human beings that require all the same things you require. Being human is a bitch for anyone seeing people as less than. For so many of us, living in a state of separation was learned over time. Some of us have eventually forgotten who we actually are. We have lost our connection to all of life and to the wisdom that we are woven together. After years of practicing separation, we see "other" people as less than ourselves.

If this is you, you're hurting your business.

The time it takes to engage with each person with a sense of wonder is invaluable. Whether or not people give you new insights depends on your receptivity. If you're in a dialogue, ready to play around with ideas and probe each thought to find out what's behind the thought, you will find value. It may or may not become a "cost savings" or a system-wide opportunity to streamline the customer experience, but if you don't do this on a routine basis, you will never get to the gem that awaits.

This practice of being present with every single person you are working with, and making sure you move around the company to engage with people you once ignored or avoided, will change your life and the life of your business.

EXAMPLES

LEVERAGING PEOPLE

One of my friends has been working to improve how world trades are managed. She is a powerhouse! Her relentless approach to creating the right solution to solve the actual problem is rare. Most of the people around her have earned the same Ivy League degrees and theoretically have the same skills as she does. What she's learned over the years is how many of her peers and bosses cover up their lack of knowledge through bravado. They "made it" by leveraging people, both in terms of leveraging their relationships with alumni friendly to their fraternity or sorority and by taking credit for the work done by their team. This dog-eat-dog world of valuing political savvy over actionable intellect is one of the silent killers of business potential.

THE ARSONIST AND THE FIREFIGHTER

Another deadly sin of business as usual is creating a hero culture. This addiction to creating problems so you can solve them often goes unnoticed. Management teams get used to recognizing the "hero" when a perceived risk is found and managed. Over time, more people play this game because they see it gaining recognition and promotion.

It eventually turns into gossiping about another person that creates doubt in their abilities. This sickness grows as well when it goes unrecognized or is accepted as "the way people are."

I've had the pleasure of taking over several businesses caught up in a culture of creating fires to put them out. When I pointed out the practice to my teams, in most cases they wanted examples; of course we all ask for proof. And in a few cases, they agreed and were "on board" to change the "culture." Changing these behaviors is extremely difficult when they have been there since the dawn of time. And no one has the power to change another person's beliefs or behaviors.

To relearn how to run a business without a hero culture, you have to unlearn leadership. Healthy businesses crave freedom. If you are the leader or one in a role of leadership, you have to begin with yourself. What are you doing to fuel this destructive and unproductive behavior? And what are you doing to free up people to be their best?

CREATING LAYERS OF MANAGEMENT

Times were good. The business was growing rapidly and the trips and lavish dinners were never questioned. It felt great to finally be working in a business that seemed to be moving forward instead of turning around businesses that were struggling to make payroll.

There were *layers of management* and endless meetings to get the pulse of what was going on. That didn't feel good. It quickly became clear that at a certain level in the organization, everyone was an interpreter, and most interpretations were skewed. Communicating took a herculean effort as the layers created a kind of telephone game. By the time those at the top got the message, it was anything but true and accurate. Most of the people filtering were into the political games, and the best among them were also the best at protecting their personal brand. Some of them expanded their power to protect their favorite people. None of it made sense. Growing your business requires speed to action. This overlayering slows growth and, over time, kills morale.

Only add people between people when it's necessary. And for God's sake, give the power of decision-making to the lowest level. Be rational in determining what and how this works, but know that the telephone game doesn't work.

I was hired to consult for a friend of mine. She was running

HR for a publicly traded company and wanted my help to figure out why they were losing talent. I did the research and presented what I found. In a conversation with the president of the company, I shared with him that he was the problem. My findings clearly suggested the middle managers were not passing along vital information.

The president had created a culture of only telling him what he wanted to hear. Most of the experienced middle managers had spent decades keeping information from the president, given that this was the unspoken expectation.

He was appreciative of my candor and invited me to speak to all the managers at a national conference. I said yes and I shared my top three takeaways, and then asked if there were any questions. I'm guessing there were around eighty to one hundred people attending, and we got into a fantastic conversation. Everyone was hungry to be heard.

Since it "felt" like a success, I was asked to follow up with another round of research. Wanting to detect if there was any follow-up commitment on his part, I asked if he had adopted any new measures to address what I'd recommended. The answer was no. Therefore, I said no.

No more than necessary, no less than required.

ONE YOU

It starts with you!

Business today: In business, we spend almost all of our time managing the "rules of flight"! This exhaustive effort to control the controllable always creeps into areas of the business that need less or no control. Creating all this busywork of *grave importance* keeps leaders from being introspective—not of the business, but of themselves. And then the business.

Today, most leaders get to One when they accept accountability for others' failures. This is somehow thought of as a noble act. It's simply a part of the well-established dogma. And in most cases, this is the closest some get to this idea of being introspective.

It's time to change your priorities. We all have grown up with limiting schools of thought. Whether these limiting thoughts are espoused by our parents, schools, or friends, they creep into our subconscious and begin to govern us.

We are *all* born curious, creative, and connected. From birth to death, we have a similar arc of experience. Early on, we only know our felt sense. Depending on the environment, some of us hold onto this wisdom longer than others. At some point, life and systems reshape us. The journey becomes one of learning more about how to fit in or get ahead. And then, one day, we are there! We have become someone we don't know—a proud moment gone unrecognized by the press.

For a few of you, this idea of not knowing yourself is odd. You may have successfully navigated the world without losing any part of your one-and-only self. You may have kept away from archetypes or playing roles enough to keep true to yourself. The other 98 percent have not; there's no reason to lie to yourself. You're in good company if you've become different people in different circumstances.

I came to the business world without any fears, in part because I had no goals to become something. I was comfortable being me. And for many reasons, I really only cared about the health of the business and the experience. I cared about the people I worked with and for, and the customers we got to know. Being a student of life, I watched management struggle to be human. These managers universally *bought in* to the expected norms of business as usual. They were being managerial.

When I moved into the top roles, I continued to be myself. The problem with being myself in a world where no one had an interest in me, and for that matter anyone, was that I was keenly aware of every experience where I didn't fit into the club. Each time I drew a different, and often opposite, conclusion than the club members, I knew my "stock" went down. Although it was disappointing to experience the groupthink, it was fine with me. At this level, most people fought for the sake of fighting. They protected their turf through aggression or position and did all of this seemingly with no self-awareness.

This comfort in *being the only person I knew how to be* changed over time. I got burnt out on the oversized, egoic archetypal characters. After turning around several businesses where an egoic archetypal leader had screwed up the business, and as I worked with yet another version of the same thing, I started to lose interest in fighting against "business as usual." Loved the people, disliked the beliefs.

Why would anyone limit performance? Of course, those who do would never see or acknowledge this fact, but it happens all the time.

It matters where we focus! It matters what we invest in! It matters that we build and manage structure, rules, systems, and the like. But we can no longer afford to spend most or all of our time in Four. From a place of deeper wisdom, we need to spend most of our time, within and throughout the organization, to become our one and only self and humanize the business. By freeing up ourselves, and then everyone in the organization, we will begin to experience the potential that emerges throughout the company and beyond.

We will find *yes* by staying with ideas long enough to find opportunity and say *no* together. We will begin to see continuous improvement become everyone's job without making it everyone's job. Fear slips back into the place it belongs, as a felt response to danger. It is no longer held for hours, days, or lifetimes. Every person really counts and every day matters.

I'm checking in on whether I've accomplished what I wanted to accomplish so far:

If I did what I meant to do by starting with Four and ending with One, you've gotten the point that business today spends most of its time in Four.

Now I'm going to imagine a future where this is no longer true. This future state means everyone spends

most of their time in One, Two, and Three. Four is important and managed, but is no longer managed through fear.

FUTURE STATE IN BUSINESS

ONE YOU

It does actually start with you!

We have to be the change! Our investment in how we show up, stay present, be accountable, relate to everyone, and leave the day examining what we can do better is our primary work!

The path to freedom is within! Once you free yourself up

to freely connect and co-create with everyone you are with, you will know. You will know why unlearning leadership is so important. It won't take too long to see the results. And if it does take longer than you want, stay the course.

It starts with you! Get to know yourself. Who are you?

No one else can answer this question for you. Others can point. You discover. This selfish decision to figure out who you are turns out to be the most selfless and courageous act any one of us will ever take in our lives. So why does this matter?

"Because."

If your answer is that you are a CEO, husband/wife/partner, rich or struggling, powerful or weak, father or mother—if you are defining yourself by the masks you wear—you are in your egoic mind. You may be a CEO that is married with kids, and express the You that is You in each of these relationships. But if you are a different person depending on whom you're with, you are not going to make a difference in the smallest of things, let alone change the world. And whether you like it or not, you are here to change the world. You are here to change the world. You are here to be the change.

From this deeper understanding of our authentic selves,

we love more deeply. We lead our teams with more heart. We create more energy that fuels more life into our businesses. We are more present and genuinely caring with everyone in our lives. Our closest and most intimate relationships grow deeper. Our weakest and most destructive relationships go away. No attachment! No detachment.

On this journey to your one and only self, you will be in the battle of your life. And this battle will be against the world's strongest foe: your repeated patterns. When you observe the egoic mind in action and simply watch it come up with all sorts of tales about what is and isn't possible, with evidence based on past proof points and future fears, you begin to see the truth beyond these limiting beliefs.

This part of you that starts to realize your ego is not you and is not real, begins to see everything as it is. You begin to experience life as your teacher, and people as a reflection of yourself. You begin to realize we are all whole and parts of the whole of life.

On this journey, you may have learned that there are personas and masks we *all* wear. You may have studied archetypes and believe that they are woven into each of us, that we are meant to be different people in different settings. I would suggest you reconsider this idea. The idea of a *felt sense*, a WBW (whole-body wisdom) approach to being your authentic self, is a more productive pointer.

These ideas of being different people in different circumstances are blocking us from our essential selves. I'm not suggesting we don't wear masks and tap intó archetypal behaviors. It just isn't necessary. I know there is a You that is aligned with All. Period.

Without doing this work, you will not have the transformative impact you are meant to have in business and in life.

You matter! It starts with *you*!

IT TAKES TWO
Everyone really does count.

Listening is not a tactic! You don't learn to listen. You do learn to quiet and find this moment without thought. From this place, you listen. Staying in this place, you engage.

You can play the game of "active listening" and likely do a pretty good job of it. But it's not necessary.

When you learn your one and only self, you learn to listen through this one and only You. From this place, you are free. You are no longer fearful, threatened, in competition, trying to one-up someone with a clever retort, or afraid of looking foolish. You simply show up, stay curious, and play with ideas. You don't practice your answer while the person across from you is speaking. You are present, attentive, and curious.

Practicing listening is like practicing breathing. When you meditate, you often focus on your breathing. This is a good thing. When you no longer need to meditate because you are present in each moment, this is the life you're meant to live.

There's nothing wrong with meditation. Nothing wrong with practicing how to listen. Just let go of the endless stories and be there in total, complete presence.

That is the practice! Give everyone your full attention.

From your authentic self, you can now be in an authentic relationship with every single person around you. You can selflessly build into them, invite them into their story, and leave room to **let go so you can know**. You come alive in wonder as you seek to uncover what that person in front of you is wondering!

From this place, you relearn what leadership really means. You relearn who you really are.

THREE IDEAS THAT WILL CHANGE EVERYTHING

It matters that your thoughts, words, and actions align

THOUGHTS AND BELIEFS

I tried finding some definitive research on the number of thoughts we have in a day. It's been a few decades since I've researched this topic. Wow! Without a ton of confidence in the number, I'll use 50,000 thoughts a day.

I then searched how many of our thoughts are negative and how many are unique. *Psychology Today* suggested that 70 percent of our thoughts are negative. Deepak Chopra says around 95 percent of our thoughts are repeated. I'm not entirely confident in the source of this data either. It is a great pointer.

The current trend is to focus on having fewer thoughts. I agree with this notion, to some extent. Even if this is a good direction to head in, my curiosity wonders how to have more unique or new thoughts. How can we shift our thoughts from negative to something other than negative?

Pause and consider this: we all have been rummaging through old negative thoughts all day. And, for that matter, every day. To make matters worse, most people believe they have more positive thoughts than they do negative. So where are your thoughts going now?

WORDS COUNT!

I was in my early twenties and listening to NPR. On this particular day, I heard something that changed my life. To this point, I'd been frustrated by my educational experiences. I knew what I wanted to learn and, in this pre-Google age, I'd found no "education systems" that would help me explore my endless curiosity.

I finally found a university that "sold" the idea of "designing your own degree." It turned out that I could only choose a few different classes. For the times, this was an "innovative" idea. Even today it would be considered innovative. Thirty-two years later and almost no progress. All the *innovative* ideas are nothing more than a different version of the same damn thing. I quit.

I was hungry to learn and knew what I wanted to explore. So I started on a new journey, reading everything I could find in my circle of interest, and then expanding to read whatever that openness created. The bookstore became my home away from home.

Back to the NPR segment I heard that changed my life: I heard the word "autodidact."

Since I heard this in the context of the speech, I had a good idea of what it meant, but still needed to look it up to be sure. I found a way to name how I showed up in this life. I was and am a *self-learner*, or *autodidact*.

Imagine this: You are now on this journey within to understand whether your beliefs are born in truth or wired by fear. You begin to see your thoughts and question the inner dialogue that judges others, creates separation to maintain power over others, and is the source of any one of the millions of thoughts that separate us from each other.

And in place of this old thinking, you emerge: The you that now activates critical thinking in those around you. The you that is profoundly curious and passionately driven to make each moment count, encourage each person, and connect with each customer. This "new" You is the You that you were all along. A mouthful for sure—and *true*.

You simply needed to remove the stories keeping you from getting back to "You."

From this place, you are changed and everything around you changes. From this place, you are on fire about life, business, potential, and what's possible, and even curious about what each person thinks. From this place, your thoughts and words activate because they are aligned.

You no longer rehearse the crap out of your presentations to those working for you; you simply share what is important to share. **You let go of knowing your audience for the naked truth of knowing yourself.** And from this place, you no longer use platitudes, understandably tough to do, in place of purpose.

Example: I was a VP, and the CEO spent the better part of a day teaching how to get "buy-in" on a new product. He led us through a decision tree, and once we'd completed the work and he'd written it all up on the whiteboard, he flipped the board and showed us how he'd manipulated everyone into his idea. He basically said he got buy-in by making it our idea. I asked, "So what happens when they learn you're full of shit? When they no longer trust your intentions?" He laughed and said, "It works. Trust me!"

I've heard endless versions of this same buy-in approach over the decades. **No more buy-in!**

Most managers and executives create value statements and the like to build a culture. Words without meaning are simply words. Those creating hollow concepts support their efforts by stating, "I want people to feel like we care." And I ask, "Do you want them to feel like you care, or do you care?" Words count!

ACTION IS ALIGNING

Getting to the You that is You is work. Choosing to "be the change" means you live the words.

When your beliefs align with activating words, you now walk into the business world—and all of life—anew. You are free. You are powerful. You are transformative. You are alive.

FREE THINKING IS...

A free thinker is one who

- Forms opinions on the basis of reason
- Thinks independently of authority or dogma
- Evaluates with the requisite complexity before drawing a conclusion
- Shifts from fear to favor, moving into problems with resolve until there is a solution—and then sees the solutions as the potential next problem

Once you've come back to You, aligning words and actions is easy. It really is. It may not be popular or comfortable, but it's easy. Coming from a place of freedom, you tap into the perfection of living in alignment with life.

FOUR RULES OF FLIGHT

The rules matter, but only in relation to the purpose.

I am not an aerospace engineer, and for the sake of this point, I am going to simplify the story to illustrate my point. Birds and airplanes can fly because they knowingly or unknowingly use the four "rules" of flight. They don't have the luxury of adding a rule or taking one away. The outcome would be tragic if they did. It is what it is.

Apply this to your business now. Is your business over-burdened with policies, rules, and expectations that keep people from doing their best and most impactful work? I'll bet I could go into your business and find the choke points that you can no longer see. Perhaps you created them due to a rogue employee doing something harmful. You may defend the decision even in light of the fact that, let's say for the sake of this argument, 99 percent of the people did it the right way.

Be careful when adding barriers based on fear and risk. They both lie to you all of the time. Data are seldom linear. Life simply doesn't work out in a neat, packaged way. It does point, though.

First, keeping it simple doesn't mean dumbing it down. Having said this, how do you simplify your business processes, practices, and policies? Start by using what I'll call "beginner's mind." Try seeing every detail like it is new to you. Invite others to do the same.

So what are your rules of flight?

Let me give you an example: When I turn around businesses, one of the first things I do is study process. While I also learn people—to discover what inevitably turns out to be the central problem—I have found that process for the sake of covering your ass kills businesses as fast as dehumanizing the business or not aligning the business with a clear purpose/vision/idea. And I've learned that people hide bodies in process. Really!

In the end, broken leaders create broken systems, so it really is always a problem of leadership.

I pull groups together and begin the process of stripping away stupid policies. I inevitably learn what the legacy leaders assume is happening because they sent an email four years ago, and expected then and expect now that this dictate somehow became a rule or policy. Even at the board level there are historians that state, "I know we said this cannot happen again. Why didn't anyone set this expectation? Someone needs to be fired for this!" You get the point.

There is inevitably an argument about what constitutes a policy and whether or not it should always be followed. My simple approach, which is never simple in practice, is this:

There are *rules*. These are nonnegotiable. They are written to be in compliance with laws, governing bodies' expectations, and the like.

There are *policies*. Policies are there to frame decisions. They are not in place to make decisions. If the person in charge of making a decision decides to make an exception, fine. Document, describe, and do. Practice transparency without judgment. When a person starts routinely using their logic over the policy, one of two things needs to happen: recommend removal of the policy or write a new one.

There are *best practices*. This is the social fabric of a healthy company: everyone exploring, innovating, and creating incremental efficiencies that apply across the company, all shared and adopted for the right reasons. *It works!* And, if it doesn't, don't do it.

Four should take up the least amount of time in most people's day. Get your arms around this mess and you will find savings, improved customer experiences, happier employees, and a whole lot more. You may even find yourself changing as you let go of fear, ego, and the desire to control. You get all of this without letting go of the discipline it takes to adapt to the ever-changing environment and the need to measure everything!

Start making damn sure you are adding barriers or layers for actual business reasons. Start throwing away stupid and reactionary policies and expectations that were developed to protect you from the minority of people doing stupid things. Design your business *for* the right people doing the right things in the right way and allow this to be an expression of each individual.

No more than necessary. No less than required.

WHAT IS GOING WRONG?

Seemingly nothing, if we look to the various news outlets. Most of the news points to Wall Street or Warren Buffett's annual report (my personal favorite). Of course there is an endless supply of talking heads touting their wisdom and using a variety of leading indicators to both create fear, so investors hold cash, and attempt to spur opportunity to incentivize action.

Things are going well and the markets are working as they are meant to work. True?

In an era of "big data," we seem to be continuing the age-old practice of using data to support our beliefs. The downside of data is that they can tell a whole bunch of misleading stories. It seems the smarter the leader, the more relevant the old quote, "Liars figure, figures lie." The only thing worse than bad or incomplete data is no data. So data today are really a leadership problem.

By the way, I've learned to play the same game. At times I've spent days trying to find the data to position a conversation. Let the data tell a story. Unfortunately, when I came up short, I kept playing with more data to find a story worth telling. The purpose was to explain an unfavorable trend in the best possible light. My preference then, and my recommendation now, is to let data do their job. Our role is to stay curious and keep looking for the relative truth. No need to feel or believe anything. Embrace curiosity.

Why would any rational human being try to manipulate the data? They wouldn't, is the answer. This brilliant and flawed system needs an overhaul. Getting to the requisite complexity in pursuit of the truth is a blend of science and free thought. What and how we measure is far too linear. Linear data are nearly useless. "Big data" are almost as useless. Smart data require more than degrees and information. They require a different definition of "smart."

WHAT IS SUCCESS?

Success is earned on all levels by investing time to go within. Learning how to let go, to surrender the comfort of *knowing* to return back to all that life offers, is where we start again. This is success: Starting anew again and again. Expressing our curiosity, ready to co-create, and wired to stay connected. Allowing the experience to be our teacher and being present with every person, every day.

From this definition of success, businesses experience improved results by looking at the outcomes as nothing more than a measure of the inputs. On the journey to business success, you will go through a process of relearning this lesson. Accurate data matters! Using data right means no games, no emotion, and no judgment. At some point, when people hide behind the fact that liars figure and figures lie, you will say good-bye. Support them on their next journey and move on. There is no room for games in success. This is tough to swallow for the businesses creating cushion so they'll make their bonuses.

In this model, you run the risk of firing people that you used to promote. They are addicted to being the hero, looking good, and "winning." Success has no room for foolish, self-serving games.

Success in business is felt by everyone as they learn to be successful together. No more beating up operations and then going out for drinks to celebrate success while operators feel like failures. No more!

Success feels damn good for everyone because it takes every single person to get there. Success has no problems with failure. Good and bad days are just two different kinds of days. The human experience has everyone *all in*, and in turn, you are *all in* with their lives. Success is finding "yes" when it's the right thing to do and using every ounce of support to get to the right "yes" and the right "no."

What matters most is being present in a free-thinking state. Being able to not attach or detach, but connect and create. This definition of success goes beyond trust, beyond the words of the day like "resilience" and "transparency," and into the naked truth that neither exists. They both emerge from your genuine nature. They cannot be harnessed or manipulated into something you want. If you're selling this shit-show, it will not show up in the outcomes!

My call to action for every single person leading or aspiring to lead a company is to avoid using these words to "get something" out of people. Instead, trust in the slow release of your limited self for the transformative experience of being yourself. This is the one and only place where all the meaningful words live. From this place, you get the best of every single person!

Our greatest successes are measured by building into each other and our society. This meaningful life as a creator, leader, and contributor will become the business of our future—one where 80 percent of people are fully engaged. One where 100 percent of people know their value and express it through all they do. This pursuit of excellence will expand potential and grow businesses in a new, more meaningful way.

You can have fun! All the time. Even in tough times, you will hold onto the joy of life. You can fail without repercussion and learn without fear. You can treat people with kindness. All the time. You can love your company, some or all of its people, and yourself, for doing good and doing well. You can be in the wrong place and work together to get out or get to the right place. And you can struggle for a season and fall apart. You may or may not get through this period in the same company or role—the point being that it is not through threats or fear that one or the other result happens.

Time to learn how to free up your thinking! Stay in a state of curiosity. Wonder out loud what is possible. Find "yes" by staying with the "no's" until you get there or they go away. Don't measure everything by time, cost, or return! We destroy the outcome of so many things by placing a timeline on them. Time everything that needs timing! Understand the value of every investment or cost. Measure the cost in relation to the reason; not everything has a financial return. And with great discipline, grow, grow, grow to earn healthy outcomes.

I'm going to start by focusing on two simple ideas. These two ideas plague our businesses and our lives. Each of these ways of being in the world matters a bunch.

First, we cannot create any lasting change without first coming to terms with "others." You and I have to get beyond the scoring of good and bad people. We must learn to walk into every interaction being our fully realized selves and inviting the person in front of us to express her fully realized person. We need to see others as equal human beings, regardless of their stories.

Second, life gets in the way. A lot! Reacting to bad decisions with anger, judgment, or threats doesn't work. These shallow actions need to be replaced with "Because."

When a product launch blows up, and the team didn't recover in time to make it look good, there's nothing you can do about it. From a state of acceptance or "Because," you can recover. By not reacting or limiting the chance to learn, and with an openness that allows everyone the freedom to be self-critical and share critical feedback, the learning is learned. The life lesson is accepted. And no one leaves the situation with a scar.

Let's dive in!

OTHER

Each story matters. Everyone—everyone—matters.

Unfortunately, there will be no shortage of exceptions for the judges among us. Headline news: we are all in this chosen role of judging one another with self-righteous indignation now and again. More often than not, our judgments are petty. Whether these judgments are shared with all your friends and repeated to all who will listen, or just quiet critical thoughts, they sap energy from you and seed *Otherness*.

On the other hand, most of us have had the experience of letting go in order to actually consciously know we are woven together. In this consciousness, we may even have a memory where we acted on this Truth. Rare as these moments are, they do help us see the *Truth beyond our beliefs*. This Truth is simple. There is no Other.

Why not play around with the notion that every single person is worthy of your love and nonjudgmental presence? Can you imagine a day when you accept every person as he or she is and allow for his or her unfolding without your mind adding to or subtracting from him or her? Nothing too magical here. Just start where you are, and be aware of the employees, coworkers, and customers around you; be aware of the waitstaff, dry cleaner, and person walking by you; be ready to meet your friends, family, and community where they are. Come from a loving presence, committed to each person you have chosen to bring into your life, and get real.

Choose to walk into the story of your life ready to accept that you created this story line. This easy process has proven to be nearly impossible to unfold. I really have no awareness of why this is so, but it is. It is very difficult if your story has exceptions and judgments about certain people, behaviors, or beliefs, but here you are, ready to start again and again. Until one day...voilà. You are there... and then you're not. Ugh.

Choosing to see others as separate, and thus separating yourself from others, is the birth of war. This war of words and violence is birthed in collective "Otherness." Buying into the notion of binary thinking of good/bad, right/wrong, smart/dumb, left/right, and so on turns into binary actions. The collective insanity of shared beliefs that pit one group against another group is perhaps one of society's greatest illnesses. I am simply saying: come to this consciously, choose to see it for what it is, and then own it. **When you allow yourself to understand this practice in a deeply personal way, you will be your own teacher.** Actually, you will be tapping into *a deeper truth*, which is ever present and there for everyone.

What are the odds that we will all stop the madness of

creating Other? Could our collective choice to live in a co-creative way to change the world actually change the world?

What if I told you that math is our friend on this journey of believing the exponential growth that will come from our oneness? Math really is everywhere in terms of translating what is happening in the world of "energy" created by *oneness* or *Other*. Energy vibrates at a quantifiably higher level in some of us, and within each of us, it vibrates at different levels in different circumstances. What would the math of energy tell you about yourself? Could this expression of quantifiable results become the gateway for the millions turned off by learning math in school? I think this type of math can become a language that truly teaches us the power of our thoughts and the consequence of our limiting beliefs.

How about this? Regardless of your political beliefs, your bias toward self-reliance or social welfare, and the endless list of ways you have chosen to separate, can you start with yourself and your path toward the people you experience, and play with this idea that we are all kindred spirits?

To the point: the Other is You! We are all "Other" to someone. All you can do is be You. And when you are You, love is the primary language. You may be asking, "Why bring this up?" Because when someone else judges you, I want you to start being aware of his or her projection onto you; if you accept him or her, you become Other. Be *in the moment*. I'll bet you can have some fun today with people who drive you crazy. No one else defines You. Be You, and others will move into themselves, for better or worse.

From this place of one in love, every single option is possible, even the tough ones. When you act in *right action*, you do not personalize the action (a Buddhist philosophy). You simply act from love, and then you are present again in this radical honesty I see as the start of "getting it."

Being honest with yourself and then others—to then be present in all of life as it is—takes one choice. From this moment where you are awake to your observer nature (oneness), acting on it in relationship (kinship), and not attaching to any situation but simply engaging in it, this one choice is another perfect definition of real power!

By the way, acting from a place of pure love, there is no Other.

Side note: A part of choosing to love, regardless of the circumstances, is also choosing to say "no" and go. Coming from the inside out, this choice can be grounded in love and respect, without judgment or attachment. If the energy or conditions are not right for you, learn to move. It's good for both parties, which, voilà, is One.

But do not create a story about moving away from someone. If you do, you are back to Other. Stick to the facts and hold a loving presence, regardless of the circumstances. This way, you will stay with being You. And the person or people you walk away from will be whomever they choose to be.

In the United States, we are drowning in Other.

In a nutshell, creating Other gets ratings, wins elections, judges international leaders, and drives business. The news cycle keeps the masses in a state of judgment about "other" people or "other" businesses or the "other" political party they disagree with, although they often have no clear reasoning for their own beliefs. We are all getting mired in this noise of nonsense and making enemies of our neighbors.

Try not fueling Other. You may see things happen that you never thought possible.

BECAUSE

What if we could answer every question that comes up about why things happen the way they do with one word? Since there's no dramatic pause necessary, I'll cut to the chase: "Because." Regardless of the circumstances, this is a perfect internal answer. Why do good people do bad things, people behaving badly do good things, and well-intentioned people screw up?

We know change is constant, people are predictably unpredictable, and life is unrelenting. Given these facts, it is wise to accept the "deed" once it's done. If we don't accept what is, we begin to make a bad situation worse.

BUSINESS STORY

A cross-functional team was redesigning the enterprise system and, in this effort, they were debating the merits of the following: a single-system, best-of-breed approach and price (ROI). A year into their research on the top solutions, they scheduled several presentations to discuss meeting either or both objectives. They decided that price would not be considered in the first round.

The group was ready to present their initial findings and recommendations. During the presentation to the larger executive team, they couldn't answer several simple and important questions. Frustration grew throughout the day, as the data were a copy of each sales pitch, without further detail. Everyone had been checking the box on presenting three options and hadn't gone deep enough to present and support each with detail, giving the group three viable options.

There were plenty of mistakes made along the way. The easiest to see is that there was no "along the way." Fifteen months into this and there were hundreds of untold useless hours spent doing what? And why didn't they meet quarterly with updates on progress?

Answer: The group met routinely. This should have been enough. But it wasn't.

Another obvious problem: The executive team's motivations were price and improved controls. Although pricing was communicated as one consideration, it was framed as a return on investment. So, no one working on the project used these two expectations as they were intended to be used. Starting the project on the same page should have been an easy first step.

Why did this happen? "Because!" It was clear, after the presentation, that the group needed to start over again. And it was clear that the executive team had no interest in starting over. And since they didn't begin again in a state of Because, they scrapped the project for the next fire. Bad decision!

Had they not given up, but rather explored the many points of failure and returned to the project ready to accelerate with a clearer vision, the project would have lived or died on the merits of its value. Accurate math is never the problem. People do two things: they use math to support their idea, and they overlook the requisite complexity. Math, like life, is neutral.

Learn to accept the unknown and be open to unlearning, and you may just find yourself present! In this presence, your mind will benefit from acceptance of what is, or a presence where you neither attach to nor detach from what is. You have arrived at Because.

Because is the most freeing answer to the intellectual unknown or unknowable. And eureka! You knew all along. What is there to know? Let go and you may find the answer to this simple question.

In every single situation, life offers us a chance to free up our mind and wonder. When we choose to accept Because as a starting point, we immediately tap into our deepest state of curiosity.

In contrast, many people live their lives *knowing*, and in their knowing, they shut out potential. They trust in their personal beliefs and power over their felt sense and hearing the many voices. They give in to limitations, separation, and control as the safest path forward. They stop seeing life as our teacher and ignore the gift of Because.

Let go of what you think you know—even if it is an absolute truth for you. Let it go! You can always come back to this place once you've experienced new ways of seeing the same thing.

Staying with your initial belief is perfectly fine, as long as you do not attach to it. The best way of knowing if you are attaching is that you feel a need to defend it. The Truth needs no defense, but our beliefs do.

Each time we ask "Why?" and stay open, we learn, and the Because takes shape. *Letting go to know*—this work of not attaching to anything—really is the practice. Each Because is a gift that moves in accordance with what you create within. One, Two, Three—*go*.

One: Question.

Two: Accept what is.

Three: Just listen with curiosity.

From here, you move beyond belief to potential. The back and forth in a trusting connective dialoguing, debating, or dancing within and around ideas will emerge. It really feels good, doesn't it? Test this process of nonattachment, being careful not to detach, and allow the creative space to unfold.

Side note: Acceptance is not agreement or giving up. It is

a simple state of allowing different opinions to be equally true. From this powerful place, the future or unfolding of this conflict will often have brighter days ahead.

Go to bed each night reviewing the gifts of the day, and speak into the wisdom gained. Be thankful you are waking up! Fall to sleep in acceptance with an intention or two. Your night will pick up from there, and odds are you will move into a deeper subconscious state capable of quantum shifts. And then, the gift of gifts is waking with a smile. In joyful gratitude, you embrace the intention of your upcoming day.

If you think affirmations or intentions equal "self-help," you are right. That is, as long as your thinking is not aligned with the derogatory judgment of self-help. If it is, stop—you need it most. Self is the right place to be. And from your one and only self, you will help everyone you encounter. It's as simple as this.

Hint: Find the "one" thing you can't seem to let go of. Write down the reasons why, with all the colorful language in your self-talk. Then, sit quietly with a new thought. Imagine the "one" thing in your life that brings you calm, deep loving feeling, or excitement. Write down why this is so. What makes either set of reasons true? Which story gives you life, and which story takes energy away from you? Go through the bad and good stories and explore whether your beliefs are real. If they are real, does this reality need your repeated attention? If you find they are not necessarily real, can you move away from giving them power by laughing at your attachment to the beliefs? Perhaps you can accept what they are without defining why. From here, you might be able to use the pointer Because.

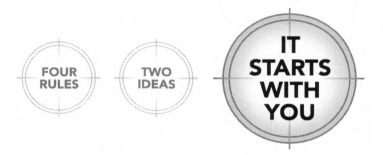

Our lives today are compartmentalized. We are attempting to be the right partner, parent, friend, family member, or worker. All of these roles, including many more, are simply roles. Yet we give in to them as we attempt to please or control (obvious extremes). No one on earth is a parent, friend, lover, partner, or worker. We are not a role!

To the extent that you play a role by being yourself, you

diminish your value. You are not a concept. Your value can only be realized by being your one and only self. When you finally let go of the endless stories that limit you, in favor of the truth beyond these limiting beliefs, you are finally in the presence of your self.

We are meant to be significant! And we can now be what we are meant to be!

Again, in our true nature, we are connected in a powerful, even transformative, way to everyone around us. We ignite together when we are together.

When we stay in the role of being the many separate versions of ourselves, we are more selfish. We are reacting to the competition for our attention and time. We are not our one and only self.

We are all here to accelerate, co-create, and live a transformative life. Yet almost no one discovers this beauty and creates this energy that is woven into each one of us.

For God's sake, wake up! Leaders, get out of your damn ego and wake up! Let go of the endless beliefs about control, power, fear, and whatever limiting thinking comes with your beliefs to live into your profound, life-transforming power. Use your drive to connect humanity. Use your deep intellect to grow rather than control. Give everything you've got that so many people don't have, for the good of humanity and the success of your business.

THE TRUTH STARTS WITH YOU!

So, who are you? Are you the sum total of your roles? Do you find your truest self in the work you do and gravitate toward this expression of yourself as your greatest joy? Is your belief in organized religion guiding the definition of who you are?

Why are you here? Are you here to get wealthy and enjoy all that money and power can buy? Are you here to create businesses, raise kids, or sing? Are you here to be a healer, be a counselor, or play sports? Are you here to tell stories?

It really matters that you get to the truth of these two questions. My bet is that when we each wake up to our fully realized self and do what we are meant to do, the world will change for the better. This discovery does not come from a workbook you buy and complete. It is a journey of discovering your *felt sense* and learning to trust this whole-body wisdom over your ego and fears.

When you get to know yourself and then show up as the You that is You, everything changes! And from this place you connect, create, and ignite your curiosity. From this natural state, you accelerate into your reasons for being here, now. You co-create with a free spirit. In this felt sense, you embrace life in all its pain and beauty. From this selfish act of taking enough time to figure yourself out, you love more deeply, live more consciously, and give more freely.

Answering the question "Who am I?" is the single most important and courageous journey any of us will ever take. And you have to make the decision to start. Thus, it starts with *you*! Why not start today?

BUSINESS OF LIFE

Every single business problem turns out to be every single marital problem and parenting problem, and the problem within each role you play and each mask you wear. They all tie back to a lack of understanding yourself and the impact you have on people around you and, ultimately, our world.

When our actions don't match our thoughts, or when

they do, and our thoughts are filled with fear, nothing of lasting value is created. It may feel good if you are the leader creating fear to drive performance or to make sure everyone knows who's boss. Know that both the feeling and the results are temporary, and your felt sense is all ego. If that sits well with you, then I guess some people are here to divide us, limit business potential, and keep others away from their potential.

If you can't see the point of shedding these controlling tendencies for real power, stay with it. In the end, you may see more of what you want in the business of life that you can bring back to the life of business.

The data clearly show that most of us are not engaged at work. Employees the world over want more from their work experience and it seems they actually want more out of life. When we awaken to the potential awaiting us and become the change people are asking for, we all benefit.

LET GO TO KNOW

While it is clearly true that everyone has the power to own their story and live it fully, not every person has the equal ability to impact the whole company. For this reason, when you are given the great gift of leading, owning, or playing a top management role in an organization, take stock. This message is exponentially more important, given the fact that you set the tone.

No matter what your role is, and specifically if you are an executive leader, **let go to know. Let go of your school of thought for a new teacher.**

Your new teacher is listening, being present and curious, loving, and learning. Your teacher is debating without the need to "win" but with the desire to teach and then learn. You will assume the best in everyone once you start this course. And when someone falls short, you will pick them up and work to get back on track.

You will eventually learn that your teacher is *life*. Your teacher is everyone you meet and every situation you're given. Each layer of egoic beliefs you shed reveals a new set of limiting beliefs, until you eventually open up to what is possible. You begin to consider the idea that we may just be better off working together than apart.

This battle is with our ego and the extraordinary power we've given this machinelike brain. Our lives are controlled by the egoic patterns we repeat over and over again each and every day. We are the sum total of what we think. You may want to tattoo this on your wrist if you are processing the world through your egoic mind: "I am what I think!"

As we've learned, we spend almost no time on positive or unique thoughts. In a state of separation from ourselves, and therefore everyone else, we fuel disengagement. We will never have the "trust" of our team or company because we come from a place of distrust.

Thankfully, we have a choice. We can trust in this *felt sense* that taps into our WBW. These bodies of ours are wise enough to heal themselves, know the unknowable, and expand beyond the limitations born of our egoic patterns.

So why do we resist trusting this wisdom? Why would we prefer to give our power away to those around us who want it? There are two ends on a spectrum of choices to process this world: egoic patterning on one end, and our WBW on the other. Your choice matters!

Our *egos* are filled with endless limited and limiting "truths" we tell ourselves. Throughout our lives, we invest an enormous amount of energy into building the case for our beliefs, born within our own egoic minds. For most of us, the list of beliefs we defend as "the truth" or "the way it is" grows stronger and, eventually, these beliefs show up as symptoms in our bodies. The longer we attach to and defend our limiting beliefs, the higher the likelihood our symptoms will turn into unmet potential, hopelessness, and, ultimately, life-threatening illnesses.

This attachment to our beliefs literally kills us. Our limiting beliefs kill innovative ideas, kill our creativity, and kill our energy. We end up trusting this egoic mind over ourselves.

Thankfully, we have a choice. We all have access to this intelligence born of our oneness, grounded in our shared humanity, and awaiting our choice to wonder long enough to say "Yes!"

Our *felt sense* aligns our heart, stomach, and brain with the source that unites us all in the universal intelligence. Our WBW goes far beyond my ability to express, but points to the fact that we have intelligence within each cellular structure and in the space between.

When we are in ego, these energetic signs simply do not align. When we choose to show up in life and stay open, the rich language of spirit will guide us.

There is a field of "knowing" that is simply present for those willing to **let go and know**. *Letting go is the key to the knowing.* Moving away from trusting your egoic thoughts, you will tap into this abundant field that gives us quantum advances in life.

Back to reality. Our limited thinking comes from the world of time and space. In this well-studied world and near-universal practices, we have become living clocks.

Telling time in this complex world is important to us. We live today for the future and hold onto the past, leaving little to no room for the moment. Our WBW has little room to come alive in this machinelike world, fueled by our ego.

Our collective ego has created massive systems that, by design, cripple innovation and reinforce mediocrity. We're too busy to understand this because we are counting: Counting the time it takes to get something done or measuring the length of time on a call to increase efficiency. Measuring the behaviors of customers to increase conversions/revenue. Using data to make decisions without a keen understanding of the requisite complexity and the right weight given to things that cannot be measured.

Leaders hold onto their hopes and fears and invest enormous energy in both states, which unintentionally creates management confusion about priorities, and then operational confusion soon follows.

Whether you lead a Fortune 500 company, sit on the board, or are an entry-level employee, **it starts with you**! It starts when you decide to come alive.

As you allow yourself room to let go of your limiting beliefs and embrace the space that opens up in this newfound freedom, you will begin to play! This emergence of your authentic story will grow stronger and inform you through your whole-body wisdom, a felt sense.

And then one day it will hit you that you are free. You will finally understand the simple fact that you are designed to be free.

These moments turn into days and become a life worth living, because you've come alive! You've uncovered what you knew all along. You are simply here to be You! Beyond roles and stories, you find your authentic self, one story expressed in limitless ways.

ACT from this place, and the business of life will transform the life of business.

LIFE SOURCE

How can we be so far off? We have been at war for thousands of years in the name of God. We have burdened ourselves with guilt over our sinful nature. We have successfully created a world devoid of our oneness as we unite behind our unifying belief in separation. Yet we pretend to do all of this for the good of people.

What is the *source* of all this insanity? Are you able to avoid the news, or if you do read or watch it, can you accept the news as drama, rather than some version of reality? Better yet, do you have a long view of these times and see them in the fullness of cycles, of which this moment in time is behaving in a predictable way?

Perhaps it could depend on where you grew up, your social class, and whether you rely on society to inform you or you choose to inform yourself. You may find that from your view of life, there are many sources at play. You've given up on one unifying source, or you never bought this narrative in the first place.

I've spent a great deal of time listening to and reading a wide variety of perspectives and have come to this realization:

No one has it right! No one knows! And yet, it is all knowable. But you have to let go to know!

BUSINESS

What is the *source* of the most successful and sustainable companies or innovations in the world? Is it leadership, stable sectors within the market, or a relentless pursuit of excellence? Can we use the wonderful book *Good to Great* as one way of answering this question? Or is the research too focused on all the right things? The author studied what he could see in the data and learn from conversations, but is there more to know?

I suggest the source of our greatest business successes are freethinkers. This will be the topic of my next book, given the importance of exploring this misused and, at times, poorly defined term.

In general, this idea of freethinking is tied to the use of logic, reason, and data. This notion of a freethinker is that of one who is a nonconformist, independent of authority or tradition, and fiercely independent. This may sound counterintuitive, and it excludes the following description of a freethinker.

Reason born of our unifying mind taps into a field of knowing. This requires quieting, meditation, or some form of intuitive knowing (WBW) outside of reason and logic. Woven together, our world is gifted with another freethinker. Business is transformed through our ability to freely think.

SPIRITUALITY

Many philosophers and spiritual teachers resonate at a high frequency as they speak and write about pointers that awaken and connect us.

Some of my favorites are Hildegard von Bingen, Eckhart Tolle, Rumi, Jesus, John O'Donohue, Mark Nepo, and Lao Tzu. I also find the conversations between scientists and spiritual devotees moving. David Bohm and Jiddu Krishnamurti had one of those odd and powerful collisions of thought. Mitch Horowitz writes masterfully about esoteric new thought leaders. William Henry masterfully explores ancient art and artifacts coupled with the written word to expand meaning. His work reminds me of Joseph Campbell's lifetime exploration of mythology.

There are literally thousands of books worthy of your time. Although none of them is as powerful as the journey within, the right pointers for each of you can be found. They can help you in some way or another to begin.

Jon Kabat-Zinn is one thought leader around mindfulness practices. In the practice of zen meditation, you are guided away from finding the answer by releasing the question. Letting go or being present moves into a constant state of being. This journey to a continuous state of presence is best described by Eckhart Tolle. Spiritual explorers can inspire our curiosity, seed new possibilities, and leave us wanting more. And we still have to come back home (to our own body) and experience all of this ourselves.

Do not follow anyone.

Everyone seems to be selling something, even when it's nothing.

The truth is within us all, and no one—*no one*—knows your path. Some may have more wisdom, and when they share their wisdom openly, without trademarks and prescribed steps, you will be in the presence of a "field practitioner." They teach and allow everyone to play off their ideas, which I call "pointers." They know that our deepest truths are unifying and cannot be harnessed. The truth has always set us free, and this is only found within.

My preference is a direct relationship with *source*. I've gravitated toward mystical journeys as the strongest evidence of our direct relationship with our shared source. From this place, I know the power of free thought and the sense of freedom within that isn't reliant on other opinions.

Our workbook called life is filled with lessons. These lessons are neither good nor bad as they relate to source. They simply present themselves on our journey. However you choose to read or listen, or whomever you choose to read or listen to for insights and pointers, you need to go back *home* and tap into your "felt sense," your whole-body wisdom, for a taste of the truth beyond beliefs.

Accept that there's nothing to prove or get out of this life in ego. Live it fully and honestly. One person's path is going to look strikingly different than another's, with one thing in common: they choose to either serve our greater good and elevate the human condition, or they don't. In both choices, they are part of the same light, expressed in differing qualities.

Don't get caught up in words. Keep finding ones that resonate with you, and work to express yourself. Then let go and know. Let go! And *know*.

SELF

Who am I? There are many answers to this question as we choose to invest in learning who we are. The I that I am is a paradox of sorts, as the answer is within the question. Why, then, do we collectively live our lives with answers that are not accurate?

Because we have abandoned our inner journey for the perceived value of our outer experience. Nearly every human-made system reinforces trusting the endless external answers, at the cost of going within.

When was the last time someone asked you who you are? When was the last time you attended an organized religious event and were pointed toward your direct relationship with source, versus someone's interpretation of scripture? When was the last time you sat around with friends or family and helped each other learn to let go of limiting stories?

When you make this deeply personal decision to explore who you are, everyone around you that is not on this journey may discourage you from finding the answer. Most of our relationships are about getting something from each other. When you stay the course and shed the need to wear endless masks, you regain power.

From this place, you are, without question, more of everything that unites us and less of everything that divides us. Your energy or power is shared freely and this body wisdom will no longer enable or compensate when people want you to be their story of you.

They are stuck in their egoic mind. You are not!

"Ego" in Latin means "I." The term as we use it today is said to have originated in the early nineteenth century. Some say the word points to qualities that are good, some say it points to qualities that are good in measure, while others consider the ego a barrier to our true self. The psychotherapeutic version of ego is interesting, and points to its role of mediating between conscious and subconscious thought. According to Oxford Living Dictionaries, we derive a sense of personal identity from our ego.[*]

Ego is up for grabs, as far as I am concerned. Wayne Dyer

---

[*] *Oxford Living Dictionaries*, s.v. "Ego," accessed April 27, 2018, https://en.oxforddictionaries.com/definition/ego.

says it means to "Edge God Out." *A Course in Miracles* points to the ego as being our reminder to continue *the course* (life is the course). I kind of like the acronym Enjoy Great Orgasms.

Words anchor ideas and, before long, these ideas end up becoming enduring beliefs. We need to learn the language of our ego to understand how we get back home. This journey back to our one and only self is through our felt sense. Yes, I said felt sense. *Our body of evidence is our body.*

Ego creates the illusion that we should be in a state of fear of others. Ego teaches us to believe in limitations and the importance of being on guard. In the natural world, we experience unity, love, and abundance. It should not be this simple, but it is. Our ego tells us this simplicity is BS, with all sorts of evidence to support the judgment or attachment to "reality." *Ego* takes one of a million beautiful thoughts and twists it into something less.

But what about being self-confident? Isn't healthy confidence good?

Self-confidence is related to where you are on the journey to your *self.* And yes, it's good, but not when it's managed by your egoic thinking.

Your whole-body expression is a feedback loop. When

you listen to your own wisdom, you learn who you are. Your thoughts become your life. With a ton of patience and pointers along the way, you will find yourself alive. You will realign with life-giving thoughts.

This aliveness will continue, the flood of life happening to and around you without your ego needing to feed it.

There are many healers who have been on this whole-body journey that can help you break through your resistance. I've been around some gifted healers over the years, and I know, for some of you, this process of "letting go to then know" is too abstract. Look for a healer that will help you unwind into your body wisdom. They will not be able to do any of the processing for you. Their gift is helping to facilitate your process. The answer is within!

LEADERS

If you are aligned with your superego, as many business executives are, you have earned your successes because of your ego. Letting go of any aspect of this ego-centered identity is insane, given all the successes.

On the surface, I agree. Our ego is outstanding at creating the perception of power over other people. This power over others ensures that people fall in line. But it has little to do with power. It has more to do with fear.

One of the greatest limitations in business is fear. And the egoic leader will never know this from where they see themselves and their company.

Fear and the drive to dehumanize the business for the sake of results create mediocrity. While many of you have made millions in business relying on practices that limit potential, you have left tens of million on the table.

What will it take to trust this shift? Will it take top- or bottom-line growth? Will it show up through improved customer and employee satisfaction? Or will you find you were measuring the wrong things and learn the natural laws of excellence?

ONE SELF

Utopia is not a wished-for impossibility. Utopia is one way of seeing the truth and having the guts to speak it or, better, live it. There will be no "utopia" in ego. Sadly, it is quashed by a flood of people living in fear, and from a place of "not enough." And my use of the word "utopia" is meant to be jarring. Living into our full potential is all I'm pointing to.

On your journey within, be aware of the impact your shifting presence is having on those around you. The closer you are to yourself, the clearer you are in all you do. From here you will find your voice that is the change you want to see, the voice that knows what is beyond your intellectual knowledge.

Gandhi found himself through this lived expression of truth to be the change he wanted to see in this world. Viktor Frankl pointed us to a similar truth. He essentially said that between stimulus and response is the freedom to choose. He taught us that the most powerful motivation in human life is the pursuit of meaning.

Being your authentic self will change the world in ways that today limit the world.

Living into your full potential will expand beyond any measure of success today.

Let go of the limitless studies that say habits are created in thirty, sixty, or ninety days. This is not helpful or accurate. The timing is timeless. Just do the work if you see it as work. Or become the observer if you like the idea of shedding stories and beliefs that no longer need your attention.

Also practice nonattachment and nonresistance in this bizarre process of dying while you are alive and breathing new life into the truth that there is no death. And there really is only one You. This you that is You awaits.

Are you ready to live life as You?

WHOLE BODY WISDOM

Our bodies have three main processing centers. When we align our heart and gut, two processing centers, with our mind, the only one many of us use, we begin to tap into our power. Our modern medical framework is slow to join the centuries of knowing this felt sense, this whole-body wisdom. Thankfully, there is research being done to prove what healers the world over have practiced.

Our bodies are self-organizing systems capable of what we still consider miracles. The resistance to healers helping people through periods of dis-ease is twofold. First, we trust scientists in all their shortcomings more than we trust our felt sense. We give our power away, rather than harness the power within. The second factor is good old-fashioned greed. The trillions of dollars spent on cancer alone is reason enough to downplay and criminalize actual healing.

This whole-body knowledge is beyond our ability to process. Don't try. Our whole-body awareness is both exponentially complex and perfectly simple. Let go of needing to know how it works. Or, if you are a scientist, spend your life solving for how it works. Until you "know," you will learn in a felt sense and trust this for what it is: the foundation of your intellect. You have to experience it to know it.

BUSINESS

In our business world, we have been known to trust and then distrust our gut. Some of this ebb and flow has more to do with what we read than what we feel, as many authors both support and then debunk this idea of gut instinct.

Trust your gut! You can and will use your brain. Don't wait for your intellect to compute and your ego to interfere. Answer through the felt sense and then through your free thought. In free thought, you're able to use data, reason, and all that thinking can offer, without losing anything. This deeper felt experience is your gut instinct or felt sense.

Getting back to this WBA (whole-body awareness) will include heart wisdom and literally all your body.

WE END AS WE BEGAN...

I really do want us to change the world. It is within us to do so!

And I really do believe business has the single greatest potential for our world to collectively change for the good. I have no other reason for writing this book. In sharing my lived experience and why I've learned to trust this experience over the many schools of thought, I hope you take the time to rediscover the potential that awaits.

The end of business as usual requires that you unlearn the endless limiting beliefs and gain the ability to tap into the potential that awaits. Join me and millions of people ready to say "yeah to it all!" This phrase captured me when I first heard Joseph Campbell use it to describe the rich texture of mythological beliefs he'd studied over a lifetime. He didn't choose one school of thought over another; he chose it *all*.

ABOUT THE AUTHOR

For more than twenty years, **GUY PIERCE BELL** has
been successful in business despite his unconventional
approach. He knew early in his career that his brand of
leadership created momentum by connecting with people
to reach their full potential. He continues to trust in the
experience of staying curious over any specific school
of thought.

He now shares his passion for humanizing business by
writing, speaking, and connecting with businesses ready
and willing to re-imagine what is possible.

Made in the USA
Columbia, SC
02 August 2018